INTRODUCTION

Catfishes are a large and quite unique group of fishes. There are well over 2,000 species contained in more than 400 genera. Catfishes are found periods of time and some routinely swim to the surface of the water for "a breath of fresh air."

Catfishes can be giants among

Heteropneustes fossilis are dangerous to man since their spines contain venom which is powerful enough to kill humans.

throughout the world in tropical waters and in many cooler-water areas as well. There are two families of saltwater catfishes, but most catfishes are found in fresh or brackish waters. Catfishes are very popular in the aquarium and on the dinner table as well. Bullhead and channel catfishes are important in aquaculture as food fishes.

Catfishes have evolved to fit many niches. Some catfishes live in fast-flowing streams while others are able to live in stagnant or even polluted swampy waters. Some catfishes are equipped to live out of water for

freshwater fishes. *Siluris glanis* can grow to a length of about 15 feet. Catfishes can also be among the tiniest of fishes. Adult *Corydoras pygmaeus* measure less than $1^1/2$ inches.

Siluris glanis is a gigantic catfish which can grow to 15 feet. Tiny *kittens* are sometimes sold for the aquarium.

Corydoras panda barely reaches 3 inches in nature but it has spines in its fins to discourage being handled or eaten by predatory fishes.

Corydoras pygmaeus barely reaches 1.5 inches.

While most of us think of catfishes as bottom dwellers, there are a number of species that are mid-water swimmers. Some catfishes are quite lethargic, remaining for hours in the same spot, but some, like the iridescent shark, are constantly on the go. Some catfishes swim upside-down and some use their mouths to attach themselves to rocks in swift waters.

Catfishes are generally peaceful creatures but nature has provided them with some pretty awesome defenses. Many catfishes have sharp and sometimes poisonous spines in their dorsal and pectoral fins. To be "spined" by a catfish can mean a trip to the hospital. *Heteropneustes fossilis*, the fossil cat, is quite aggressive and their spines contain a very painful and potentially lethal venom. In the aquarium, however, they don't usually look for trouble and a little bit of caution is all that is necessary to enjoy keeping this intriguing animal. In fact, most injuries from catfishes are the result of carelessness on the part of the keepers rather than malice on the part of the

The upside-down catfish, *Synodontis nigriventris*, is found in the Congo River, Africa, where it may grow to 6 inches. It occurs in schools at night.

Brochis splendens is a robust fish which may reach 3 inches. It is very peaceful and recommended for the community aquarium.

catfishes. They simply have been equipped with defenses that enable them to swim with predators without becoming their dinner. When alarmed, some catfishes extend their fins and lock their spines rigid. Any animal that tries to swallow this little fish with sharp spines will soon think better of the idea. This defense mechanism can be a little troublesome when netting catfishes, as the spines have a tendency to get stuck in the mesh of the net. Putting the net into the aquarium water and letting the catfish swim from the net on its own usually will give better results. Trying to extricate a frightened catfish from a net is dangerous for both the fish and the handler. By the same token, when bagging a catfish, double bags with newspaper between the bags will help keep the bags from being punctured. It is better to use a plastic bucket or cooler to transport catfishes, especially on a lengthy journey.

Platydoras costatus has curved spines running along its body to protect it.

WHAT IS A CATFISH?

Variety is a key word when talking about catfishes. Generally, we visualize catfishes as scaleless fishes with "whiskers," but there's so many more different types of catfishes than is generally imagined. Most catfishes do have barbels. They use them as sensory organs to find food, in courtship, and to survey their surroundings. Most catfishes are scaleless, but some are equipped with armor plating. Some other catfishes generate electricity. This electrical charge is a great weapon and it is also used by the fishes as a kind of sonar that helps them to get a reading on their surroundings in the murky waters they call home. The catfish mouth is unique. The jaws are provided with muscles

A close up of the venomous *Heteropneustes fossilis* which clearly shows its thick whiskers.

Schilbe mystus sports four pairs of whiskers or feelers. Two pair on the bottom and two pair on the top. Whiskers are always in pairs but not necessarily in even amounts.

that make their barbels move. The number of barbels differs. Eight barbels is considered a full "set," but there may be as few as two.

The adipose fin of most catfishes is generally fleshy, but not always without supporting fin rays. It is located behind the dorsal fin, an extra fin that many advanced fishes do quite well without. In the catfishes the adipose fin points to its primitive ancestors, a feature retained from antiquity.

The dorsal fin is optional in some catfishes. Members of the small family Malapteruridae, the electric catfishes, have no dorsal fin at all. Silurid

The buffalo catfish pokes for food incessantly along the bottom of the tank. It has a fleshy adipose fin on the rear section of its back.

Pterogoplichthys gibbiceps occurs in nature (rarely) as an albino.

catfishes may have only a very small one. On the other hand, the giant sailfin dorsal of *Pterygoplichthys gibbiceps* is one of its outstanding features. The dorsal spines of some catfishes are quite sharp and part of the aforementioned weaponry.

The Weberian apparatus is a collection of four small bones that serve as a kind of a hearing aid for some fishes, including catfishes. This enhances their ability to detect sounds and vibrations in the water.

Some catfishes can make sounds. The "talking catfish," *Amblydoras hancocki*, makes sounds simply by grinding its spines in their sockets. They use their swim bladders to amplify the sounds they produce.

Pterogoplichthys gibbiceps is a magnificent South American catfish. Most aquarium catfish come from northern South America, mostly northern Brazil.

Amblydoras hancocki.

THE CATFISH AQUARIUM

Catfishes are often kept in community aquaria without regard for any special requirements that individual species may have. If they are comfortable in the generic conditions of the community tank, that's fine. If not, tough luck for those conditions and add other compatible fishes as well, that's fine. It is unreasonable to expect any fish to adapt to an aquarium that is not large enough for the species, or that does not have the right kind of water, or that contains other fishes that are not

Pimelodus pictus from Colombia in South America. This fish has a large mouth and is difficult to maintain.

the catfishes. In this book, we propose that catfishes can often be admirable community tank residents, but there are many catfishes that are unsuitable for the community tank and should be maintained only under specific conditions. If you wish to build your community tank around suitable tank mates.

Aquaria for catfishes are as individual as the catfishes themselves. Some catfishes are very small, some can grow so large that they should only be included in displays in large public aquariums. Because of the many different biotopes in which

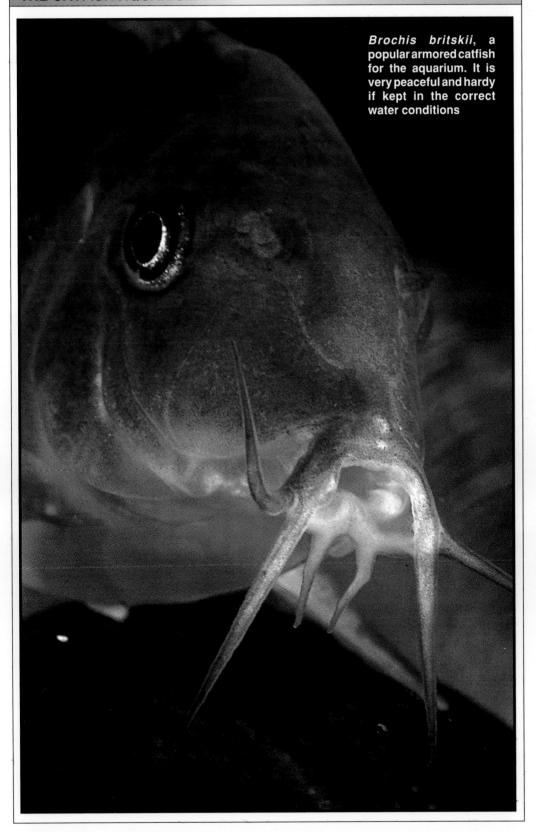

Brochis britskii, a popular armored catfish for the aquarium. It is very peaceful and hardy if kept in the correct water conditions

Acanthodoras cataphractus has long been known to science and is very widespread in South America. It is protected with curved, sharp spines which are punctuated by a creamy line along the sides of its body. Don't hold this fish in your bare hands!

catfishes are found, water conditions as well as tank setups should approximate the conditions in which they are found in nature. Catfishes are tough, though, and it is not unusual to see catfishes thriving (apparently) in tanks that would seem totally inappropriate for their well-being. It is one of our goals in this book to make sure that catfishes get a fair shake at being kept properly. We are sure you will do this once you have learned the proper methods of keeping them.

HOW BIG?

You may not believe this, but those adorable little one-inch South American redtail catfish (*Phractocephalus hemioliopterus*) that you can see in almost any pet shop can grow to over 36 inches in the wild and to a comparable size in the aquarium. This fish will soon outgrow all but the largest tanks and it requires absolutely excellent water quality as well. This example demonstrates the acute need to "know before you buy." A fish the size of the South American redtail cat certainly deserves to be kept in an appropriately sized tank and under the proper conditions. On the other hand, there are many, many catfish species that you will find in pet shops at a size of one inch that remain small and are manageable in average-sized aquaria.

The method of keeping and raising catfishes varies with their size, shape, and the species involved. The old one inch of fish per gallon of water rule has been questioned many times, especially when the calculation involves one big 20-inch fish as opposed to 20 one-inch fishes. Twenty one-inch fishes in a 20-gallon tank is not a problem; one 20-inch fish in a 20-gallon tank is. Basically, a 20-gallon tank (24 inches long) is well-suited to a small group of dwarf catfishes (especially the species of *Corydoras*, *Brochis*, and *Aspidoras*). Of course, a larger tank is never a problem. It is only smaller tanks that can create problems!

A 30-gallon tank (36 inches long) works well for up to a trio of 5-inch catfishes, like species of *Synodontis*, species of pleco-like loricariids, such as species of *Ancistrus* and *Peckoltia*, or even *Dianema*.

A 55-gallon tank (48 inches

In the Rio Negro/Rio Branco intersection of Brazil, Sr. Miguel da Silva runs a charter boat. At a small village the locals showed him this gigantic *Phractocephalus hemioliopterus*, the South American redtail catfish. This fish can be caught along the banks of the Amazon River in great quantities.

long) can very easily house a trio of your 10-inch catfishes, which include the larger species of *Synodontis*, *Pimelodus*, larger species of pleco-like catfishes, such as species of *Hypostomus*, and the black lancer (*Bagrichthys hyselopterus*).

A 100-gallon tank (72 inches or more) will house the above-mentioned little redtail catfish (at maturity) and many of the other jumbo catfishes, including the shovel-nose catfish (*Pseudoplatystoma fasciatum*) and the shark catfishes (*Arius* spp.). The large American predatory catfishes, like the channel and bullhead catfishes, are also appropriate for this size aquarium.

AQUASCAPING

Catfishes are often thought to be bottom-dwelling nocturnal fishes that spend most of their time hiding under a comfortable piece of driftwood. Just the opposite is true in many cases. There are many open-water (pelagic) species that are out and about all the time, so there is no one kind of aquascaping that works for all catfishes.

Driftwood and Rockwork

The nocturnal species prefer a tank that is crowded with driftwood, rockwork, and plenty of plants. The busy, open-water species need plenty of open spaces for their active lifestyles.

For the sedentary nocturnal species (that do get up and move

Arius jordani is sometimes called the *shark catfish* because it looks like a miniature shark.

about when the tank is dark!) think driftwood. Not only does it provide the cover that they require to feel at ease, but many of the suckermouth types graze on the driftwood and microorganisms resident on the wood, and it is thought that they even need the wood for their digestion. Avoid sharp-edged rocks and other decorations that might injure the catfishes. All aquascaping elements must be smooth and rounded to prevent injuries.

The Substrate

The most important issue when thinking about the substrate is that there are no sharp edges. This rules out completely the colored shards of glass that are sometimes used in aquaria! It's usually best to go for a darkly colored, natural gravel that has a grain size that measures about 1/8-inch in diameter. Finer sand is appreciated by species of *Corydoras*, and the problems usually associated with compaction of the sand are not really an issue since the corys spend all of their time rooting around in the sand. Larger particles of gravel have a tendency to allow too much dirt to collect, so if you choose to use this kind of substrate, you must be sure to vacuum the gravel more often than usual.

You can't have live plants without sufficient and proper quality light. Your petshop should have a variety of lamps to show you. Photo courtesy of Penn Plax,

Plants

Plants and catfishes are compatible. Catfishes don't eat aquatic plants. Some do eat zucchini and lettuce but they leave the leaves of plants alone. (If you see them grazing on plants, it's the algae they're after, not your plant.) The worst thing a catfish might do to a planted aquarium is accidentally expose the roots while foraging for an escaped tidbit.

Some of the plants that you might enjoy in your catfish aquarium include: species of *Anubias*, species of *Echinodoras*, Java fern and Java moss, species of *Cryptocoryne* and *Aponogeton*. We prefer rooted specimens over bunch plants simply because they are less likely to be relocated by the catfishes.

Dianema urostriata is one of Brazil's most beautiful armored catfish. It is a community fish.

Catfish can be messy. They stir up the bottom and pass waste through their system in copious amounts. Powerful filtration is necessary. Your local petshop should have suitable filters for your particular needs. Photo courtesy of Penn Plax.

EQUIPMENT

The kinds of filters, heaters, lights, etc., you use in a catfish aquarium depend in large part upon the size of the tank and the kinds of catfishes kept. A small species tank of *Corydoras* can be very simply furnished with a sponge or box filter and a small heater, but if you are keeping any of the large predatory catfishes, you must use heavy filtration and protect the hoses, heaters, etc., from the rampages of these fishes.

Filtration

As mentioned before, a sponge filter, a box filter, or a small power filter will work perfectly well on a small tank with small fishes. Canister filters, fluidized bed filters, wet/dry filters, and undergravel filters, alone or in combination, may be employed to maintain the high water quality necessary for successful catfish keeping. Sponge filters are air driven and provide a very high surface area for the growth of nitrifying bacteria. They are not exceptionally effective mechanical filters, but in a tank with a gravel substrate will remove ammonia and nitrite quite well. Air-driven box filters work in a similar

Above: Plants not only make the aquarium more beautiful, but they sterilize the water, add oxygen to the water and often serve as spawning sites and hideouts for catfishes. To have your plants thrive a fertilizer is required. Photo courtesy of Aquarium Products.

Left: The most valuable tool an aquarist can have is an automatic water changer. Carrying buckets of water to and from an aquarium is a thing of history! Many people use the waste water to water their house plants. Photo courtesy of Aquarium Products.

fashion, but use floss for mechanical filtration and gravel rather than carbon for biological filtration. You can put carbon in a box filter for chemical filtration, but we prefer that a layer of aquarium gravel and another layer of floss be used. The gravel should only be rinsed from time to time in aquarium water and the floss should be changed weekly. If you use carbon in the box filter, you must change it often. It is therefore better to use the carbon for a specific purpose, like the removal of medication after treatment, rather than using the carbon as a permanent filter medium.

Power filters are impeller driven filters that pass the water through a stationary medium, such as sponges, ceramic noodles, plastic "bio-balls," or specially fitted pads of poly material. Power filters work as both mechanical and

The genus *Brochis* contains three species. They are all from South America and have the same requirements for maintenance. They are semi-active with most of their activity devoted to scrutinizing the bottom of the aquarium in search of food. This species is *B. splendens.*

Hoplosternum thoracatum is a very peaceful, armored catfish which breathes air from the surface of the water. It makes a nest of bubbles for spawning.

biological filters and generally turn over the volume of water several times an hour. This is good for those catfishes that require highly oxygenated, fast-moving water.

Canister filters are packed with layers of different filtration material, e.g. a sponge layer, ceramic noodles, gravel, and even carbon. Canister filters can be packed also with chemical filtration media, like adsorptive resins that remove toxins from the water. They are heavy-duty filters that can be outfitted to carry a high bio-load.

Wet-dry, or trickle filters, are slow biological filters that maintain high oxygen levels in the water. Prefiltration is critical for mechanical filtration. Because the wet-dry filter employs a large volume of media, for example bio-balls, the filter chamber itself is quite large. Fluidized bed filters are purely biological filters that use sand as the media. As water is pumped into the fluidized bed via a power head, the sand is lifted and churned, or "fluidized." Fluidized beds have an enormous surface area for the growth of nitrifying bacteria in a relatively minuscule chamber. Some models hang on the tank but there are other, larger units that are free standing. The media need never be changed and the filter is virtually maintenance-free. A sponge pre-filter on the power head will provide all the mechanical filtration necessary to remove particulate matter and keep your water clear.

Undergravel filters are run by

Pimelodus blochi is a rarely seen catfish, though there are many other *Pimelodus* available. Usually *Pimelodus* are seasonal catches for the South American fishermen. They are not spawned commercially in aquariums.

Pangasius sutchi is an Asian species that is uncommon. It may grow to 12 inches in length and eats small fishes.

air pumps or power heads. The filter sits on the floor of the tank under the gravel (hence the name!). The gravel becomes the media as water passes through it and nitrifying bacteria convert the ammonia and nitrites to nitrates. The gravel must be vacuumed regularly to prevent overloading with organic waste. At least twice a year, the undergravel plate should be cleaned as well.

Heating

Tropical catfishes generally require temperatures in the mid to upper 70's F. The heater of choice is usually the submersible pre-set type. These are convenient and reliable. For the big catfishes, it is advisable to protect the heater with a sheath of perforated plastic or PVC pipe.

The most important factor in water temperature is consistency. A rapid drop in temperature can lead to diseases, like ich. For spawning some species, like some *Corydoras* species, however, a large water change with slightly cooler water can stimulate spawning.

Lighting

Since many catfishes are nocturnal, they prefer subdued lighting in the aquarium. This is not consistent with a rampant growth of aquatic plants. One way to overcome this problem is to provide areas of light and shade, light for the plants and shade for the fishes. Obviously, a bare tank with bright lights will stress a nocturnal fish. Be aware of the fishes' need for subdued lighting. The diurnal catfishes do quite well in tanks with bright lighting and a natural light nicely displays the reflectivity of their scales.

CARING FOR CATFISHES

While some species of catfishes are found in stagnant, and even polluted water in the wild, this is not a situation we want to replicate in our aquaria. Most catfishes are extremely sensitive to poor water quality. Many catfishes are heavy feeders and this makes routine tank maintenance mandatory.

TANK MAINTENANCE

Depending on the bio-load (number and size of fishes and their feeding habits) of the cleaned and/or replaced frequently. Power and canister filters should be serviced when the water flow is reduced by 50%. The inside glass should be cleaned before every water change. The gravel should be vacuumed and siphoned as a part of the water change. Gravel washers are ideal for this purpose. The gravel is swirled about in the siphon tube, the mulm is washed away with the water, and the gravel is returned to the bottom. Replacement water

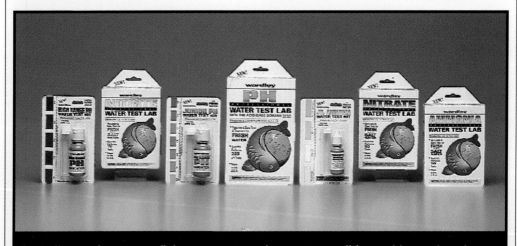

To really care for your catfish, you must monitor water conditions with a series of tests. Kits are available to test almost all the necessary parameters for both freshwater and saltwater aquariums. Your petshop should be able to supply all your test kit needs. Photo courtesy of Wardley Products.

aquarium, you must change a certain percentage of the water on a regular basis. Whether the amount of water you change is 30% per day or per week depends upon the bio-load and the efficiency of your filtration system.

Clean the filters on a regular basis. Prefilter media should be should be dechlorinated and of similar temperature and pH as the tank water.

So, how do you know how much water to change and how often? Water testing. Simple tests are available for any number of toxins in the water, but the ammonia, nitrite, and nitrate tests will tell you exactly when you must change your water. Any rise in ammonia or nitrite after the initial cycling period of the tank indicates an emergency situation where an immediate water change is indicated. Rising nitrate levels suggests that it is time for a water change.

When the tank is first established, it is natural to have ammonia and nitrite peaks. The predictable nitrite peak that occurs about two weeks after the initial setup indicates that the biological activity in the filter is progressing at a normal rate. Beyond the approximately 6-week period of cycling, ammonia and nitrite elevations are symptomatic of poor fishkeeping and increased water changes and examination of the feeding habits and fish load are advised.

Since some catfishes are naked, and without the protection of scales, they are especially vulnerable to foul water conditions. Ammonia burn, skin lesions, and bacterial infections may be caused by poor water conditions. Barbels are usually the first to deteriorate in bad water. If you notice that your corys' whiskers aren't as long as you remember, it is likely that you haven't been attending to the maintenance of the tank properly.

FEEDING CATFISHES

Catfishes don't eat poop! That said, it is true that catfishes are scavengers, or bottom feeders. Many catfish enthusiasts are offended by the perception that

Hypancistrus zebra might well be the most beautiful of all catfish if there is such a thing. But it requires special care and special food. It grows to 5 inches and prefers live foods such as tubifex and blackworms.

catfishes are workers, detailing the gravel, and cleaning up after the other fishes, but it is true. They should not, however, be expected to dine completely on leftovers. A proper diet is necessary for their good growth, health, and reproduction. There are many different foods for catfishes. Know what they need so that you know what to feed. Some catfishes are primarily herbivores that require a diet high in green matter; others are omnivores and must have meaty foods as well.

Sinking foods are necessary for bottom dwellers. These shy fishes are unlikely to come to the surface to take floating foods. For bottom dwellers, there are many special wafers, tablets, pellets, food sticks, etc., that sink rapidly to the bottom. Live foods provide vitamins and enzymes that are not available in commercial foods. Blackworms, bloodworms, tubifex worms, and live brine shrimp are the most common living foods available in retail pet shops. Earthworms can be collected from your own garden. Live foods, such as snails and small fishes, are consumed by some of the larger catfishes. Live foods are an integral part of the catfish diet and should be offered in addition to any commercial foods that you have selected. Offering a variety of foods is the only way to ensure that your catfishes will have a well rounded diet.

Bloodworms are almost universally accepted by catfish. The wood-eating catfish thrive on them as do the *Corydoras* which patrol the bottom substrata looking for food like bloodworms. Photo courtesy of Hikari.

Some catfishes are not bottom dwellers. For these species floating foods are a better choice, especially for fishes like the upside-down catfish, *Synodontis nigriventris*, that take foods from the surface of the water. Pelagic catfishes, like *Pangasius sutchi*, the iridescent shark, are mid-water feeders.

Some catfishes, like plecos and other loricariids, require fresh vegetable matter. Zucchini, romaine lettuce, dandelion leaves, and crushed peas will round out their diet nicely. Use a rubber band to attach the food to a rock or the driftwood and watch them go after it! You might want to peel the zucchini before putting it in the tank as they do not eat the tough, outer fiber of the zucchini.

Feeding Large, Predatory Catfishes

Large, predatory catfishes will accept commercially prepared foods, such as large pellets, trout chow, or even dry dog food. Strips of lean beef, chicken, and non-oily fishes will be taken with gusto. One

true with the large, predatory catfishes with mouths over four inches wide!

HEALTH CARE

Given that you have purchased healthy stock and have taken proper care of your fishes, diseases will be low on your list of concerns. Catfishes are a hardy and resilient group of fishes that are not given to catching every passing pathogen.

It is unfortunately true, however,

A close up of the head of this *Phractocephalus hemiolopterus* shows the large mouth indicating this is a predatory catfish. Most fishes will eat whatever fits into their mouths.

of the authors (R.E.G.) used to feed skinned rats to his large South American redtailed catfish! This shows that a wide variety of foods will be readily eaten by these predatory catfishes. A general rule of thumb for most fishes is that they will eat whatever will fit into their mouths. This is especially

that you may not always get healthy stock. Transportation and wholesalers' tanks are often hard on catfishes. Injuries, stress, overcrowding, poor water quality, and exposure to other diseased fishes costs many lives. Catfishes, like their feline namesakes, however, often appear to have nine lives. What would certainly kill many other fishes, catfishes usually manage to survive.

Some catfish diseases are entirely preventable. Use a quarantine tank for new arrivals. This will give you the opportunity to closely examine the new fishes. Symptoms, like scratching, rapid breathing, and injuries that may have been overlooked in the retailer's tanks, will be apparent when you examine your fish closely. A 2-week quarantine period will help prevent contagious diseases from spreading to the main tank, where they will certainly be more difficult to eradicate.

The most common health problems of catfishes are caused by environmental conditions, i.e. water quality. If the fishes are gasping at the surface, you must first suspect ammonia/nitrite toxicity and subsequent low oxygen levels and/or an incorrect pH. Cleaning of the substrate and a good water change are the proper therapies for these problems.

Rapid breathing and scratching of the gill area on aquarium objects are signs of gill flukes. Remove carbon from the filter for the duration of the treatment and use a proprietary catfish-safe antiparasitic medication. Some medications are unsafe for scaleless fishes. Check the label of the medication you intend to use. If the medication contains an ingredient that does not agree with catfishes, it should so state.

A head-on view of *Platydoras costatus* shows that the fish is very ill because its eyes are cloudy.

This *Platydoras costatus* also shows signs of stress because its tail is drooping and its fins are clamped.

Cloudy eyes and fin rot are usually the result of poor water quality that has resulted in a bacterial infection. An antibiotic is indicated in this case, but antibiotics will kill your filter bacteria, so it is necessary either to remove the filter to a safe place or to treat the fishes in your quarantine tank.

Skin wounds and torn fins can be the result of aquascaping injuries or fighting. If this is the case, observe the tank to determine how the injury occurred. Fishes sometimes like to hide behind heaters. This can burn their unprotected skin. Decorations should be examined for sharp edges. Many catfishes have very soft skin and bellies that are easily damaged. Injuries sustained in fights—territorial or otherwise—can be quite severe. The solution to this situation is that all aggressive tank mates should be removed.

Treatment of wounds may or may not be necessary. Fresh, clean water as provided by your good tank maintenance will encourage spontaneous healing of most skin and fin wounds. Keep a careful eye on these wounds to be sure that they do not become infected or develop fungus. If the area becomes reddened or appears to be getting larger, an antibiotic treatment may be necessary. The appearance of white filaments of fungus are a very bad sign and rapid therapy is necessary. Remove the fish from the tank immediately—to keep the fungus from spreading—and institute anti-fungal therapy.

Ich (*Ichthyopthirius multifiliis*) is another fairly common, but preventable and easily treated skin parasite. The infected fish scratches

Hoplosternum thoracatum are air-breathing catfish which make a nest of floating bubbles.

This is why so many fishes that looked fine in the retailer's tanks suddenly become infected when introduced to the home aquarium. Again, quarantine will prevent contagion in the main aquarium. You can treat ich by raising the water temperature to 85°F. This speeds up the life cycle of the parasite. Catfish-safe over-the-counter medications will soon destroy these parasites.

against objects in the tank and is sprinkled with white spots. Ich can be deadly if neglected and outbreaks usually follow chilling of the water.

SPAWNING CATFISHES

All catfishes are egglayers. Catfishes have some of the most diverse breeding behaviors in the fish world. Some pairs spawn and run, never to meet again. Other species are quite protective of both the eggs

A magnificent *Synodontis multipunctatus* from Africa. This is a prized aquarium fish which has been successfully spawned in the home aquarium.

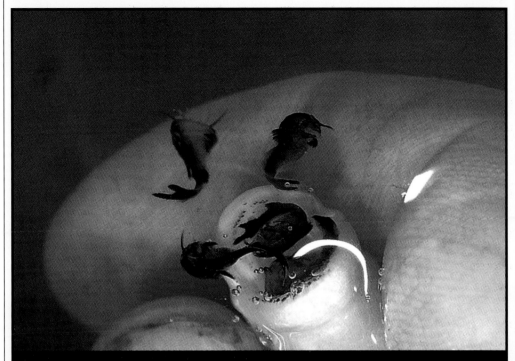

This photo shows the head of a *cichlid, Pseudotropheus zebra,* being squeezed so the fry of *Synodontis multifasciatus* are spit out.

Seven fry of *Synodontis multipunctatus* in a person's hand after they were spit out by the cichlid fish which mouth brooded them. This remarkable observation could only have been made in an aquarium.

and fry, i.e. model parents. Then there are the harem-spawning catfishes where there is one male and a bevy of females. The cuckoo catfish, *Synodontis multipunctatus*, has to be the wildest spawner of them all. It uses foster parents. The cuckoo lays its eggs with mouthbrooding cichlids who then pick up the eggs and carry them with their own. There's even a bubblenest builder, the hoplo cat, *Hoplosternum littorale*.

There are many species of catfishes that have not yet been reported as spawning in captivity. This may mean that they have indeed never spawned in captivity, or it could simply be that they are not widely kept and the aquarists who have spawned them have not written accounts of this activity. If you have had a spawning of an unusual catfish that you have never seen written up in a journal, by all means consider sending an account to *Tropical Fish Hobbyist* magazine. A photographic record of the event is desirable, but if that's not possible, try to record all the details such as water temperature, pH, and any unusual features.

Spawning Tanks

Many catfishes will spawn in the

There are beautiful catfishes and then there is *Chaca bankanensis* which has a face (with a big mouth!) that only a mother could love.

A close-up of the head of *Chaca chaca*. Its tiny eyes indicate it is either (or both) nocturnal or lives in water which has no light because its too dirty or too deep.

community tank, but predation on the eggs and young is the rule rather than the exception, so it is better to use a separate tank for breeding. The breeding tank should be bare-bottomed (without a substrate) and should have several spawning sites, such as plants, driftwood, rocks, and hollow PVC pipes. A mature sponge filter will provide some mechanical and good biological filtration. A pre-set submersible heater will keep the water at the correct temperature. The day/night cycle is important to stimulate spawning.

The tank size should be appropriate to the size of the fish you are spawning. It need not be as large as the community tank, but should be adequate for the fish and the fry.

SPAWNING *CORYDORAS*

Corys have been spawned many times in the aquarium, both deliberately and accidentally. They spawn often in the community tank, but again, it would be nearly impossible to raise the fry under these conditions. Species of *Brochis* and *Aspidoras* spawn in a nearly identical manner to corys.

Over 40 species of corys have been spawned. Mature corys are easy to sex based on body shape, especially

Above: A chubby female *Corydoras aeneus* taking a mouthful of sperm from a participating male.

Right: The female places the eggs she has been carrying in her clasped pelvic fins on previously cleaned sites throughout the aquarium.

A female *Corydoras aeneus* carrying her eggs in her pelvic fins. This may be one of the rare examples of a fish using its fins as hands!

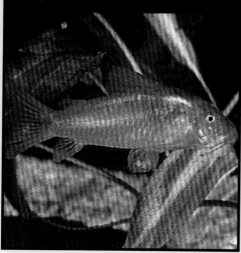

when the female fills with eggs. The mature female is usually larger than the male and she has a deeper body.

Courtship involves a lot of swimming together and attention-getting behavior on the part of the male: brushing his vent against the female's mouth and nudging her belly with his snout. They chase each other around the tank and begin to clean the surfaces of the aquarium where they will place their eggs. These could be rocks, the glass, or the leaves of plants. When the actual spawning begins, the female mouths the vent of the male, lays 2-5 eggs between her pelvic fins that are immediately fertilized, which she then places on the prepared sites. This process is repeated many times and soon the entire tank is covered with eggs.

The eggs hatch in about three days at temperatures between 77° and 79°F. The water level in the hatching aquarium should be kept relatively low, given that corys like to take mouthfuls of atmospheric air from time to time, including the fry. Baby brine shrimp is a good first food, but the fry will soon move on to mashed tubifex or fine flake foods. Be sure to keep

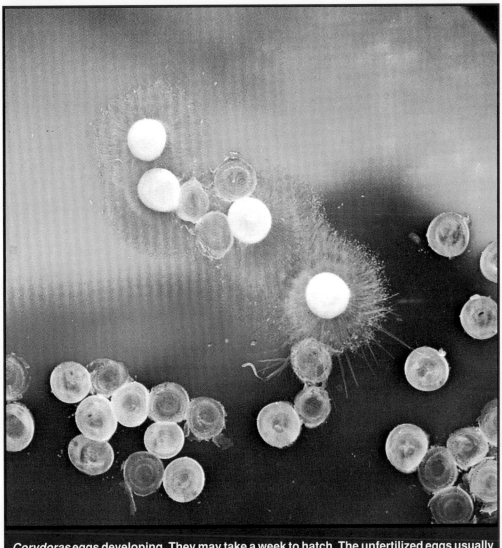

Corydoras eggs developing. They may take a week to hatch. The unfertilized eggs usually turn white in 24-36 hours. They should be removed with an eye-dropper or they will fungus as this photo shows.

changing the water with conditioned water to maintain a high water quality.

SPAWNING LORICARIIDS

Loricariids include the suckermouth and whiptail catfishes. In some species the male protects the eggs and fry while in other species the male has an enlarged lower lip to carry the eggs and the fry. Spawning methods are variable in these fishes. For the most part, these fishes are too large to spawn in the average aquarium.

There are differences between the males and females; adult males develop bristles on their cheeks. Sometimes the bristles are not obvious, and sometimes the females have bristles as well, so sexing these fishes in some cases can be difficult.

Above: In the banks of most Brazilian rivers of the Amazon area, are holes made by birds. These holes are exposed during the dry season and the birds dig nests into the soft banks of the river. When the rains once again fill the rivers, *Hypostomus* catfish take over the hole and use it in which to spawn and guard their eggs.

Ideally, these large fishes should be spawned with a 3:1 female to male ratio. This cuts down on male aggression, which can make spawning impossible with a smaller female.

Several species, like species of *Ancistrus* and *Hypostomus,* will spawn in hollow tubes. PVC pipe is a favorite spawning site as is split bamboo. This simulates the holes dug by these fish in the banks of rivers. Other species, like *Farlowella*

Below: A close up of *Surisoma panamense* guarding its developing eggs.

The developing eggs of *Sturisoma panamense.*

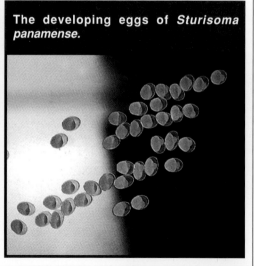

This phenomenal photo shows the *Sturisoma* using it external lips to cleans *behind* the eggs!

A *Sturisoma* sitting on the eggs. White eggs are cast aside.

Tatia galaxias have been spawned repeatedly. The adults are shown below. The kittens, shown above, are voracious eaters, especially for brine shrimp.

Synodontis angelicus is probably Africa's most beautiful catfish. It is caught at night in the Stanley Pool outside Kinshasa on the Congo River.

and *Sturisoma*, lay their eggs on the glass sides of the aquarium and on the leaves of plants.

SPAWNING SPECIES OF *SYNODONTIS*

Sexing species of *Synodontis* is not easy, and the purchase of a half dozen of these catfishes in the hopes of finding a pair is beyond the means of all but the most devoted hobbyist. The female is generally plumper and the male sports a genital extension that can sometimes be seen.

Many species of *Synodontis* have never been spawned in captivity and their spawning behavior remains a mystery. *Synodontis angelicus* comes immediately to mind.

Of the synos that have spawned, the cuckoo catfish (*Synodontis multipunctatus*) is the most well-known for its unusual and amusing spawning habits. When kept with mouthbrooding cichlids from Lakes Malawi or Tanganyika, the cuckoo catfish will spawn simultaneously with the cichlids. They rush in while the cichlids are spawning and lay their eggs. The cichlids then pick up the catfish's eggs and mouthbrood them along with their own. The catfish fry hatch in the cichlid's mouth and then turn around and devour as many of the cichlid eggs and fry as possible!

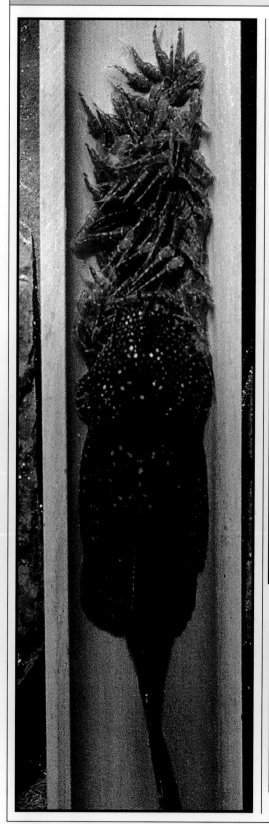

Some catfish imitate birds. They lay their eggs in hidden areas and then incubate them by sitting on them. Later they care for the kittens in the same hideaway. To the left an *Ancistrus* guarding its kittens. The top half of the bamboo has been removed for the photograph. Above: *Rinoloricara microlepidogaster* sitting on its eggs. The top half of the bamboo has been removed for the photo.

CHOOSING CATFISHES

Your catfish selection is dependent upon many things, including its ultimate size, temperament, and availability. It is a shame when people buy a small, cute catfish, become fond of it, and discover six months later that not only has the fish outgrown the tank, but the house as well!

Temperament is an issue if you are considering a catfish for the community tank. Many of the nocturnal catfishes appear lethargic during the day, but spend their nights roaming around the tank, wreaking havoc and taking bites out of their sleeping tank mates. Remember, the bigger the mouth, the bigger the appetite. Nature did not endow some catfishes with big mouths just for looks. Those big-mouthed catfishes are so equipped in order to fill those mouths with fishes. They do not distinguish between feeder fishes and prize specimens.

Availability is often an issue. Please do not be disappointed if a species you admire in a book

Corydoras adolfoi with the red spot and its imitator, *Corydoras imitator,* come from the same small stream in Brazil. Dr. Axelrod, who collected both new species says they are the same, but most scientists don't agree with him. This may be a unique instance where two different fishes can occupy the same ecological niche.

is nowhere to be found in your neighborhood pet shops. Many of the catfishes we keep in the aquarium are wild caught and seasonal, thus only intermittently available. Some are new species that are just catching on in the hobby. If there is a species you admire and want to obtain and you cannot find it in your dealer's tanks, ask if it can be specially ordered. Keep your eyes open when looking at the tanks in the pet shops. Rare and unusual catfishes are often discovered mixed in with common species.

LARGE, PREDATORY CATFISHES

Size is a critical issue. Many people like big, tough fishes but be aware that the tiny catfish you admire may one day require a very large tank and it will possibly be the only fish you can keep in that tank. Know what kind of fish you are buying before you make your decision. Consider the expected adult size, compatibility with tank mates, and any other special features of the fish you are considering. Remember that fishes grow and

that the fish in the dealer's tank may be very young and have a lot of growing ahead of it. If you are thinking about any of the large, predatory catfishes, we suggest that you consult further texts that deal specifically with the species you covet.

Among the very large catfishes that are kept in aquaria can be found Amazon redtail catfish, shark catfish (*Arius jordani*), peruno catfish (*Perrunichthys perruno*), and other members of the families Bagridae, Pimelodidae, and Ariidae. (Some pimelodids are small enough not to be a threat in the community aquarium.)

Large catfishes are powerful fishes. Be sure that you take measures to protect the equipment you have in the tank (heater, filter hoses, etc.), and that your tank cover is weighted. Many of these fish are powerful jumpers and will surely escape if the tank is not carefully covered. Every element in the aquarium must be protected and "heavy duty!"

It stands to reason that a large fish will also be a "dirty"

The predatory catfish *Perrunichthys perruno*.

The iridescent shark catfish, a pelagic species, known as *Pangasius sutchi.*

fish. You must be certain that the filter and your tank-maintenance and water-changing schedules are adequate.

PELAGIC CATFISHES

As previously mentioned, all catfishes are not nocturnal bottom dwellers. Pelagic catfishes are diurnal (active during the day) and active mid-water swimmers. They prefer to live in schools and will fail to thrive if kept singly. Pelagic catfishes require adequate swimming room to make their wide turns and fast moves. This means that they should be kept in somewhat larger tanks than other fishes of similar size.

In nature, pelagic catfishes are found in clean, swiftly moving waters. This translates into a fish that has little tolerance for high ammonia and nitrite levels or other toxins. Be sure to carry out frequent partial changes with dechlorinated water. An extra power head or air stone is beneficial.

The iridescent shark (*Pangasius sutchi*), glass catfish (*Kryptopterus bicirrhis*), and the butter catfish (*Schilbe mystus*) are examples of pelagic catfishes.

There is some crossover in the pelagic and large, predatory catfish departments.

Like the large, predatory catfishes, most pelagic catfishes will eat other fishes small enough for them to swallow. (In fact, most fishes, unless they are outright vegetarians, will eat

The huge Amazonian redtail catfish, *Phractocephalus hemioliopterus*, is not used as food by many of the locals because they don't like red fish meat.

CHOOSING CATFISH 43

other fishes small enough for them to swallow!)

NON-PREDATORY CATFISHES

Non-predatory catfishes can be easily recognized by the size and type of mouths they have. Those mouths that are on the underside of the head are designed for sifting through the substrate for tiny worms or rasping algae off rocks, plants, etc., not for devouring their tank mates. Small-mouthed fishes are not usually accustomed to enjoying meals of living fishes and, all other things considered, can usually be trusted in a community setting.

The beautiful whiskers on *Loricaria simillima.*

Loricariids

Loricariids, or suckermouth catfishes, are generally good tank residents. They are responsible for few of the aquarium crimes against tank mates, but some can grow rather large. Loricariids are South American and include such fishes as: *Ancistrus* spp. (bristlenose catfishes),

Hypancistrus zebra (zebra pleco), and *Farlowella* spp. (twig catfishes).

Dwarf Armored Catfishes

Members of the family Callichthyidae, and that includes species of *Corydoras*, *Aspidoras*, and *Brochis*, are the most benign of catfishes. They cause no trouble, do no harm, and possess tremendous charm.

Driftwood Catfishes

Auchenip-terids, like *Tatia* and *Auchenipterus*, etc., are quiet, shy types, but are not above making a meal of fishes small enough for them to swallow. They are novelties that are best kept with other peaceful fishes larger than themselves. These fishes are very lethargic and rarely leave their "home" of driftwood or rocky cover, but are very attractive to many catfish enthusiasts and have interesting spawning behaviors.

Talking Catfishes

Doradids, including such genera as *Amblydoras*, *Platydoras*, *Acanthodoras*, etc.,

Panaque nigrolineatus from South America may be the most expensive catfish in good supply. It is essentially a vegetarian and specializes in algae and rotting wood.

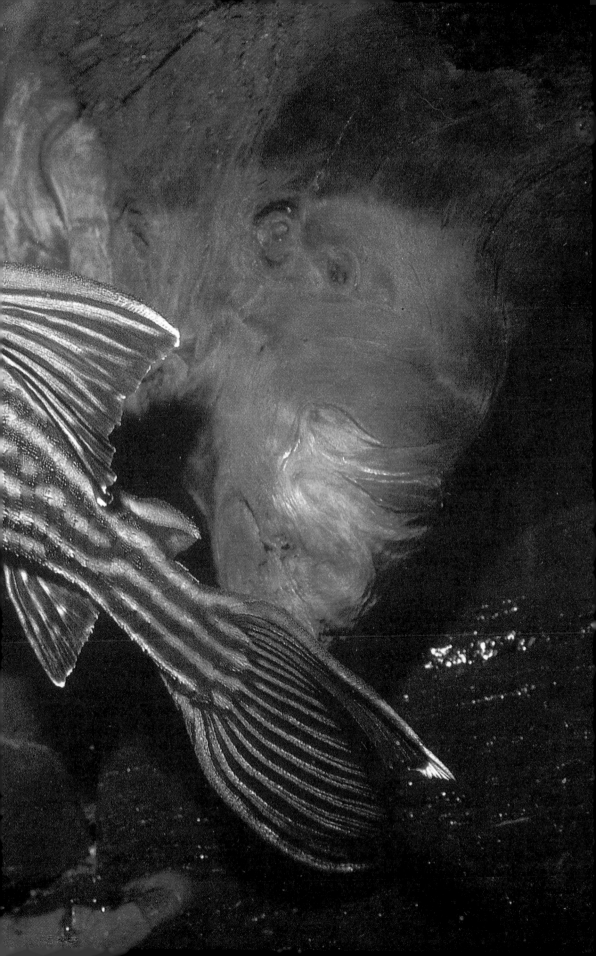

Above: The magnificent wood catfish from the Rio Xingu in Brazil. These fish are found in the bottom of rivers and streams eating away at the rotting bark on trees which fall into the water.

are able to produce sounds by the rotation of their pectoral

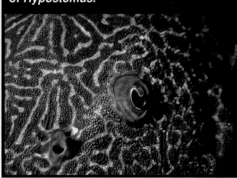

Below: A close up of the eye of a species of *Hypostomus*.

spines. These are generally peaceful, nocturnal or crepuscular (active at dawn and dusk) fishes. They like any manner of small live foods and some vegetable matter. But they are very, very shy. At the first disturbance they will bury themselves in the aquarium substrate! Be careful when handling these fishes. The catfish defense system we mentioned earlier is quite well developed in these fishes. Their spines are sharp and they move fast.

The above designations by no means cover all of the catfishes, but they put a good dent in those species commonly available through normal channels.

The *Gold Nugget* catfish, a wood-eating catfish from the Rio Xingu, has not been identified as yet.

The glass catfish, *Kryptopterus bicirrhis*.

SELECTED SPECIES OF CATFISHES

Acanthodoras spinosissimus
TALKING CATFISH, SPINY CATFISH
Range: Middle Amazon region.
Habits: Mostly nocturnal; harmless to fishes it cannot swallow.
Size: 4 to 6 inches.
Water: Parameters are not critical. Temperatures between 76° and 84°F.
Food: Live insects, worms, and crustaceans. Quality catfish food.

This is a spiny fish that can make sounds. Be careful in handling this fish as it can be very quick to lash out with its sharp dorsal and pectoral spines. It avoids bright lights, preferring quiet, secluded

Acanthodoras spinosissimus.

nooks. It will bury itself in the sand if disturbed. Use fine aquarium sand without sharp edges on which the fish could damage its soft barbels and underside. Little is known about sexual differences or breeding habits.

Agmus lyriformis
BANJO CATFISH
Range: Guyana to Brazil, coastal areas.
Habits: Nocturnal and secretive. Banjo catfishes are camouflaged when in leaf litter or under driftwood.
Size: 3 inches.
Food: Small worms and other invertebrates. Provide quality

Agmus lyriformis.

catfish food.
Water: Temperature 76° to 84°F. Water neutral to slightly alkaline.

This little fish will disappear into the landscape of a planted and decorated aquarium. It is peaceful and shy. It lies so still that it is often mistaken for dead, only to curl up when touched. Banjo catfishes are very peaceful and well suited to even the smallest aquaria.

Amblydoras hancocki
HANCOCK'S AMBLYDORAS

Range: Guianas, Peruvian and Bolivian Amazon.

Habits: Peaceful and nocturnal.

Size: 5 to 6 inches.

Food: Small live foods. Offer quality catfish foods.

Water: Neutral to slightly alkaline water. Temperatures between 72° and 76°F.

This is a peaceful catfish that is very shy. It is a hardy, long-lived fish. It will quietly bury itself in the substrate when disturbed with only its

Ancistrus lineolatus
BRISTLENOSE PLECO

Range: Columbia and the upper Amazon.

Habits: Peaceful except among males of the same species.

Size: 5 to 6 inches.

Food: Live worms, algae and other vegetable matter, and quality catfish foods.

Water: Clean and well filtered. Temperatures between 70° and 80°F.

Bristlenoses (*Ancistrus* spp.) are quite odd looking and have many devoted followers simply

Amblydoras hancocki.

eyes exposed. It is one of the talking catfishes. Males have spots on their bellies and more pronounced hooks on their dorsal and pectoral fins; the females' bellies are whitish. Pairs build a nest of detritus, cover the eggs, and guard the nest.

because of this oddness. The bristles are more developed in males and are used as sensory organs. These fish are quite hardy and resistant to disease. Provide plenty of hiding places to encourage the fish to come out into the open. They are most likely to be seen when

Ancistrus lineolatus.

they know they can rush to cover when necessary. They are super algae eaters and must have vegetable matter in their diets. Spawning is common in the aquarium with the eggs being laid in caves or PVC pipes.

Arius jordani.

Arius jordani
SHARK CATFISH

Range: Coastal Peru.
Habits: Large, predatory.
Size: 24 inches.
Food: Omnivorous but prefers meaty foods.
Water: Brackish, clean, well-filtered.

Unless you are willing to devote a very large aquarium to these fish, you will be keeping only juveniles. They are territorial among their own kind, but relatively peaceful among other like-sized fishes. The pectoral spines are quite dangerous as they contain a venom that causes wounds to heal very slowly. In the wild, they are mouthbrooders with the male brooding the eggs. They have not spawned in aquaria.

Aspidoras pauciradiatus
BLOTCH-FIN ASPIDORAS
Range: Central South America.
Habits: Peaceful.
Size: 1.5 inches.
Food: Small live foods and quality flake foods.
Water: Extremely clean and well filtered. Some current is recommended. Temperatures between 72° and 77°F. Soft, acidic to neutral water.

Species of *Aspidoras* are among the most benign of the little fishes you can keep in a community tank. Just be sure they are not harassed by boisterous tankmates. They are somewhat delicate and require

Aspidoras pauciradiatus female, swollen with eggs.

Aspidoras pauciradiatus male.

careful aquarium husbandry. They will spawn readily when given plenty of Java moss and Java fern and good conditioning foods.

Brochis splendens
SPLENDENS
Range: Upper Amazon.
Habits: Peaceful.
Size: 4 inches.
Food: Small insects, crustaceans, worms, finely chopped beefheart and other aquarium foods.

Brochis splendens.

Water: Temperatures in the low to mid 70s F. Sensitive to salt in the water, but otherwise neutral water conditions are acceptable.

There are three species in the genus *Brochis*, *B. britskii*, *B. multiradiatus*, and *B. splendens*. Splendens is the most commonly available species, but the keeping requirements are virtually identical for all three species. Species of *Brochis* strongly resemble those of *Corydoras* except that they are larger and have more rays in the dorsal fin. They are peaceful, sociable fishes that do best in colonies of ten or more.

Brochis britskii.

Chaca chaca
FROGMOUTH CATFISH
Range: India.
Habits: Nocturnal, peaceful, but will devour any fish it can get into its mouth.
Size: 8 inches.
Food: Live foods (especially earthworms), frozen foods, and pellets.
Water: Temperature about 75°F.
This is a lazy, nocturnal

Species of *Chaca*, like this *C. bankanensis*, are nocturnal, but beware of its fish-eating tendencies.

A pair of *Brochis Splendens.*

catfish with a huge mouth and a healthy appetite. Treasured for its bizarre looks, the frogmouth's most interesting feature is its huge mouth. This fish seemingly can eat fishes bigger than itself! Give it a shady, well-planted tank and put out the "Do Not Disturb" sign in the daytime, but a peek into the tank at night will reveal an eating machine. Don't take chances with any but very large tank mates for the *Chaca*.

Corydoras aeneus
AENEUS CATFISH

Range: South America from Trinidad to La Plata.
Habits: Absolutely peaceful.
Size: 2.5 to 3 inches.
Food: Corys eat almost every kind of aquarium food. Tubifex or blackworms are special treats and very good for conditioning spawners.
Water: Fresh, salt-free water that is neutral to slightly acidic. Temperatures between 72° and 80°F.

Corys are the best-loved of all the aquarium catfishes. They harm no one. They are comical little fellows that every now and then will give you a "wink" (or what looks like one). They are busy workers that use their sensitive barbels to test every surface in their search for food. It is an abuse to treat corys as scavengers that are expected to serve as vacuum cleaners for the tank substrate. Make sure that you offer appropriate (sinking)

Corydoras aeneus.

foods to the corys. They do not eat the excrement of other fishes and in a busy community tank that is properly fed might not get their fair share of the food.

The barbels of a healthy cory are well defined and well developed. Stubby barbels are the result of poor tank maintenance or the use of sharp-edged substrate material.

There are many species of *Corydoras*. They are all from South America. There are many color patterns, some slight variations in size, and slight variations in preferred water conditions, but basically they are all very similar. For more

Albino *Corydoras* species, probably *C. paleatus.*

information about the different species of *Corydoras*, consult T.F.H. Publication's TS -183, *Colored Atlas of Miniature Catfish—Every Species of Corydoras, Brochis and Aspidoras.*

Dasyloricaria filamentosa
WHIPTAIL

Range: Central eastern South America.

Habits: Generally very peaceful, but males of the same species can be aggressive toward each other.

Size: Up to 10 inches.

Food: Algae, vegetable matter, and quality catfish foods.

Water: Temperatures between 75° and 84°F; neutral to slightly acidic water.

Whiptails are often employed as algae eaters, but must be offered other types of food as well. Though a slender fish, like most semi-vegetarians they have large appetites and need a bit of variety in the form of live worms and

Dasyloricaria filamentosa.

prepared foods. These fish are very fond of hollow tubes. PVC pipe is ideal for their purposes, be it as their territory or to use as a spawning site.

Dianema longibarbis
PORTHOLE CATFISH

Range: Peru and Brazil.

Habits: Peaceful, active, and a bit nervous.

Size: 4.5 inches.

Food: Accepts a wide variety of aquarium foods.

Water: Temperatures between 74° and 80°F.

These fish are midwater and bottom swimmers but quite capable of jumping out of an uncovered tank. They prefer to be kept in schools and can be quite jumpy if startled. The tank should

Dianema longibarbus.

be clean and well filtered, but need not be overly large. A pair will do well in a 10-gallon tank, but a school of ten would appreciate a 30-gallon tank.

Farlowella gracilis
TWIG CATFISH

Range: Northern South America.

Habits: Very peaceful.

Size: 8 inches.

Food: Algae, vegetable matter, vegetable-based aquarium foods.

Water: Well-oxygenated, soft, aged water.

Twig catfishes may be long, but

Farlowella gracilis.

their body mass is very small. They prefer a somewhat deeper aquarium than most other fishes of their size. They must have plenty of plants, algae, and very clean, well-oxygenated water. Light is not disturbing to them, so a bright aquarium that produces plenty of algae is excellent.

Hoplosternum thoracatum
PORT HOPLO

Range: Northern and central South America.
Habits: Peaceful.
Size: 7 to 8 inches.
Food: Brine shrimp, tubifex worms, and just about any other aquarium food available.

There's nothing fussy about the port hoplos. When they live in muddy, oxygen-poor waters, they simply take breaths of air from the surface and pass it to their hind guts where oxygen is taken up by tiny blood vessels. When the oxygen levels get too low in the wild for even their comfort, they just travel over land (for short distances) to a more hospitable body of water.

Their spawning is noteworthy. The male (usually)

builds a bubblenest. The nests are constructed mainly of plant bits and bubbles. When the construction is complete, the female lays eggs that she carries to the nest in her ventral fins and deposits in the nest. The eggs are secured to the underside of the nest with more bubbles provided by the male. The male or both the

Hoplosternum thoracatum.

male and the female guard the nest for the four weeks it takes for the young to be able to leave the nest.

Hypancistrus zebra
ZEBRA PLECO

Range: Rio Xingu, Brazil.
Habits: Secretive, shy. Tend to be territorial among themselves. Peaceful among other fishes.
Size: 5 inches.
Food: Tubifex and blackworms. Quality aquarium foods including meaty foods should be provided.
Water: Slightly hard and alkaline. Temperatures between 78° and 82°F.

This is a relatively new fish that has taken the hobby by storm. To a large extent these fish are opportunistic feeders. They need

Hypancistrus zebra.

to have their food presented to them where they live. They can learn to venture out into the tank and compete for food but they will virtually always return with it to their caves. They can be taught to eat out of your hand, but you have to practically starve them to make that happen. Once they have grabbed a piece of food, they drag it back into their hiding place to eat it. They are not vegetarians. They are omnivores that require meaty foods that are delivered right to their immediate vicinity.

When they are ready to breed, the females commonly lie with their heads in the cave and most of their body and tail out. By curling their bodies, they lead the male into their cave to spawn. Mike Reed, a former T.F.H. editor, reports that when his male died suddenly prior to spawning, but after some courting activity, the female went repeatedly to his cave to look for him and was very agitated for a long time.

These fish are strongly nocturnal. They need to be provided with many rock caves, driftwood, and live plants. The more cover available to them, the more likely you are to see them often. When they are in prime condition, the white on the dorsal and tail fins turns bluish and a reddish color develops on the caudal peduncle.

Hypostomus plecostomus
Pleco
Range: Panama to Uruguay.
Habits: Peaceful, except that they will remove the slime from laterally flattened fishes like discus and angelfish. Sometimes aggressive toward their own species.
Size: Can grow to 24 inches in very large aquaria.
Food: Meaty aquarium foods, algae, other vegetable matter. Provide vegetable-based aquarium foods.
Water: Slightly hard, alkaline water preferred. Temperatures 76-82°F.

There are many species of *Hypostomus* that are sold under the common name "pleco." The main differences seem to be in the color pattern. They are also likely to show individual differences even within the same species.

Plecos are often kept for their excellent work on algae problems. Since a pleco can clear a tank of algae in a very short time, be sure that you offer good vegetable-based foods after the algae is gone. A big pleco has a big appetite and must be specially fed. As with any nocturnal fish, the

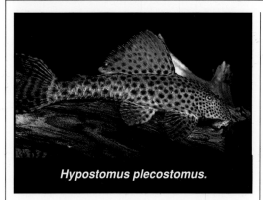
Hypostomus plecostomus.

food should be introduced to the tank just before the lights are turned off for the evening. Driftwood is also important to plecos. They will rasp away at the soft, outer surfaces of the driftwood. The cellulose in the wood is necessary for their digestive processes.

Do not keep large plecos in a community tank with skittish fishes. Their nighttime wanderings will only disturb the sleep of the other fishes. A large pleco can appear quite threatening and they are very active on their nightly forays around the tank. Two large plecos can be quite a problem if they haven't been raised together. These are territorial fish (among themselves) and can cause damage to each

Hypostomus plecostomus albino. It was found in Brazil.

other and the tank decorations if they both happen to want the same spot.

Ictalurus punctatus
CHANNEL CATFISH

Range: United States, from the Great Lakes to Florida and Texas.

Habits: Peaceful at small sizes, but voracious feeder (=predatory) at larger sizes.

Size: Up to 36 inches in nature.

Food: All foods, both live and prepared.

Water: Clean and well-aerated. This is not a tropical species and tolerates water

Ictalurus punctatus.

temperatures over 68°F poorly.

Channel catfish are novelties in the home aquarium. They grow far too large for any but the biggest of aquaria, but they grow rather slowly and juveniles are often kept by hobbyists. The problem is what to do with them when they have outgrown their tank. They must not be released into local ponds, streams, etc. It is illegal to release any fish into the wild in most, if not all, localities.

Kryptopterus bicirrhis.

Kryptopterus bicirrhis
GLASS CATFISH
Range: Thailand to Indonesia.
Habits: Peaceful and timid. Must be kept with others of its own kind. Should not be kept with fishes that will intimidate them.
Size: Up to 4 inches.
Food: Live and prepared aquarium foods.
Water: Temperature 76°F. Slightly alkaline and slightly hard water.

These are nocturnal fishes that need plenty of shady places in the aquarium. They also need to be kept in groups. A single glass catfish will not fare well at all. Avoid boisterous tankmates. They enjoy spending the day quietly resting among the broad leaves of plants. These are midwater swimmers and will not feed from the bottom of the tank, or only rarely. It is best to use a worm feeder when feeding tubifex or blackworms since these fish will not sift through the gravel for the worms as will most other catfishes.

Their tail-down posture is a normal swimming position and not an aberration. These are very quiet and very peaceful fish. They are not delicate, however, and will prosper and live long under the proper conditions.

Otocinclus affinis
DWARF SUCKER CATFISH
Range: Southeastern Brazil.
Habits: Peaceful.
Size: 2 inches.
Food: Eats a variety of aquarium foods and does a credible job

Otocinclus affinis.

of removing algae from aquarium surfaces.
Water: Soft, slightly acidic water with temperatures between 75° and 80°F.

Algae removal is the specialty of this little fish, as its small size permits it to do the detail work that would be beyond the capabilities of larger catfishes. Heavy planting and good lighting will help ensure that this little fellow will have plenty of surfaces to work over for algae. This fish or a pair of them in a large tank will mind their own business and are visions of industry.

Their spawning habits are much like those of species of *Corydoras* and a pair will produce many "kittens" if the conditions are just to their liking.

Panaque nigrolineatus.

Panaque nigrolineatus
ROYAL PANAQUE

Range: North-central South America.

Habits: Aggressive with their own kind; peaceful toward other fishes.

Size: 10 to 11 inches.

Food: Omnivorous. Will accept meaty foods in addition to its vegetable requirements.

Water: Temperatures between 74° and 82°F. Slightly soft and acidic water is necessary.

The royal panaque and its cousin, the blue-eyed pleco (*Panaque suttoni*) are real "wish-fish" for catfish enthusiasts, especially when they are young. Young panaques tend to be more attractive than older fishes, which tend to lose some of their striking patterns.

Panaques grow into large fishes. The water should be clean, of the proper chemistry, and well-filtered. As large fishes, they have prodigious appetites and produce a great deal of waste. Don't underestimate the degree of hostility they harbor toward others of their own species, so any tank that is to remain peaceful should contain only one panaque.

Parauchenoglanis guttatus
AFRICAN FLATHEAD CATFISH

Range: Cameroon; Congo Basin.

Habits: Nocturnal and shy, but will eat other fishes small enough for it to swallow.

Size: 10 to 11 inches.

Food: Everything!

Water: Temperatures between 74° and 80°F. Avoid extremes of pH and hardness.

Parauchenoglanis guttatus.

This fish is a predator with a ravenous appetite. It will spend its days hiding out beneath rocks and driftwood and become active at dusk. It will soon clear a community tank of small fishes in a typical "whodunit" style, but it is not aggressive as such. It may take a little while for a newly acquired fish to realize that there is food available in the tank, so try to offer food at dusk in the general area of the catfish. They are well equipped for self-defense with strong, sharp spines, so avoid handling these fish whenever possible.

Phractocephalus hemioliopterus
SOUTH AMERICAN REDTAIL CATFISH

Range: Amazon River and its tributaries.

Habits: Predatory, but not aggressive.

Phractocephalus hemiolopterus.

Size: 36 inches.
Food: Eats everything!
Water: Very, very clean, soft, and acidic.

Don't even think about purchasing a South American redtail catfish unless you are prepared to make a large (and long) commitment. There is no tank too large for this fish—anything less than a bathtub is too small and our usual household bathtubs are too narrow!

For some reason—and that reason can only be demand—juvenile redtails are often found in pet shops these days. These fish are best left to public aquariums and specialist hobbyists who fully understand what keeping a redtail involves. It may seem like a good idea to purchase a redtail of six inches, but a year later (if it survives) that same fish will not only be eating you out of house and home, but it will need excellent water quality and huge quarters. Keep them only in your dreams!

Pimelodella gracilis
SLENDER PIMELODELLA
Range: Northern Amazon region into Venezuela.

Habits: Nocturnal, predatory.
Size: 7 to 8 inches in captivity.
Food: Carnivore that requires meaty foods.
Water: Neutral water with temperatures between 74° and 80°F.

These fish are very active at night. They are greedy feeders that will not hesitate to remove smaller fishes from the aquarium.

Pimelodella gracilis.

Pimelodus pictus
ANGELICUS PIMELODUS
Range: Columbia.
Habits: Peaceful and very active.
Size: 4 to 5 inches in captivity.
Food: All aquarium foods taken eagerly.
Water: Neutral; temperatures between 72° and 75°F.

The common name of this fish "angelicus" also is used to denote a much more expensive and rare fish, *Synodontis*

Pimelodus pictus.

angelicus. Since *P. pictus* shows a similar pattern in reverse, e.g. white with black spots as opposed to the black with white spots of *S. angelicus,* its common name was given to it in reference to the true angelicus catfish—not a bad thing, but somewhat confusing to beginners. Aside from the spotted patterns, there is no relationship at all between the two catfishes.

The angelicus pimelodus is readily available in most pet shops year 'round. This is an active fish that is said to be nocturnal and crepuscular, but is often seen swimming around in the daytime. It's a hyperactive little fellow that always seems in a rush to get from one place to another. It is a good eater, but not likely to assault its tankmates—unless they are very small and tasty looking.

Platydoras costatus.

Platydoras costatus
RAPHAEL CATFISH
Range: Middle Amazon region.
Habits: Nocturnal. Likes to bury itself in soft substrate during the day.
Size: 5 inches.
Food: Quality aquarium foods, live foods.
Water: Temperatures between 75° and 84°F. Neutral to acidic water.

The Raphael catfish has been in the hobby for a long time and is a favorite of catfish enthusiasts. While they are nocturnal in nature, they seem to be possessed of typical feline curiosity and eventually spend good parts of the day investigating the aquarium. They are hearty eaters and not known to cause trouble to their keepers. These are hardy fish that are often found in the most inhospitable conditions in the wild.

Pterygoplichthys anisitsi
SNOW KING PLECO
Range: Paraguay, Brazil, Peru.
Habits: Nocturnal.
Size: 30 inches in the wild, smaller in aquaria.
Food: Meaty foods plus vegetables.
Water: 75° to 85°F, neutral to acidic water.

Members of the genus *Pterygoplichthys* are often mistaken for species of *Hypostomus.* The most obvious difference between the two is the more extravagant dorsal finnage

Pterygoplichthys anisitsi.

of the *Pterygoplichthys* (they have more dorsal fin rays). There are "new" species of plecos being discovered regularly in South America and many of them are quite attractive, some even spectacular. Often they are available commercially before they have been scientifically described and carry luscious sounding names like: mango pleco, gold-nugget pleco, and the like. They are often quite expensive until they have become established in the hobby (and sometimes even long after they are generally available). The snow king is one of those majestic fishes that commands a high price and is eagerly kept by many aquarists.

Generally, the keeping requirements and personality of this fish is the same as for all others of its type. Feed them well. Give them plenty of privacy. Avoid keeping them with others of their own kind. And turn the lights down low.

Synodontis angelicus
ANGELICUS SYNODONTIS
Range: Zaire basin.
Habits: Peaceful, nocturnal.
Size: 8 inches.
Food: Omnivorous, offer high quality aquarium foods.
Water: Slightly acid to neutral, medium-soft; temperatures between 72° and 84°F.

The angelicus synodontis is another one of those "wish" fishes. In 1955, the price per specimen was over $300.00. The price has come down considerably, but this is still an expensive and somewhat rare catfish. Fortunately, they are hardy and long-lived in the aquarium. Perhaps because of their price, people tend to take better care of them than they do a $1.99 cory! Be that as it may, the angelicus synodontis has never yet been bred in the aquarium despite the intensive efforts of many professional aquarists.

The angelicus synodontis is not difficult to keep. As with so many other catfishes, it craves good food, lots of sheltered areas in the aquarium, and clean water of the proper chemistry and temperature. The angelicus is well able to defend itself. It is not unknown for an angelicus to engage in a jaw locking contest with a much larger fish over a desirable piece of aquatic real estate. If this occurs in your aquarium, it is time to add some more driftwood and caves! We have

Synodontis angelicus.

Synodontis multipunctatus.

never known an angelicus to start a fight, but they will certainly hold their ground when necessary!

Angelicus cats, besides being very beautiful, are amusing creatures. They do not find it at all necessary to swim upright and will often be seen swimming upside-down, especially if there is some desirable foodstuff floating on the surface of the water.

Synodontis multipunctatus
CUCKOO CATFISH
Range: Lake Tanganyika.
Habits: Peaceful, nocturnal.
Size: 10 to 11 inches.
Food: Omnivorous, provide high quality aquarium foods. Especially fond of snails and crustaceans.
Water: Hard, alkaline; temperatures between 72° and 84°F.

This is the famous cuckoo catfish whose breeding habits have gained it such notoriety. As mentioned earlier in this text, this is the fish that "tricks" cichlids into brooding its eggs. Other than this unusual behavior, the cuckoo catfish is not much different from other species of *Synodontis*. They thrive on good care and enjoy the company of their own species.

Synodontis nigriventris
UPSIDE-DOWN CATFISH
Range: Congo basin and its tributaries.
Habits: Peaceful, nocturnal.
Size: 3 inches.
Food: Omnivorous, provide high quality aquarium foods.
Water: Slightly acid to neutral, medium-soft; temperatures between 72° and 84°F.

This fish is very odd. It swims upside-down. Other *Synodontis* are known to do this when the mood suits them, but this fish swims

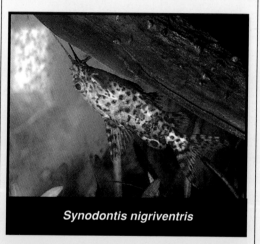
Synodontis nigriventris

upside-down most of the time. Rightside-up is unusual. This habit suits them well, as they like to skim insects from the surface of the water. Even their coloration is reversed to accommodate this practice. Where most fishes are dark colored above and light below, the opposite is true in the upside-down catfish, a camouflage that protects them from predators (birds) that would quickly snatch them from the water's surface.